Presented to

Pastor Dick

By

Ron + Lois

On the Occasion of

Birthday

Date

7-22-00

Pastor Dick

Ron + Lois

Birthday

7-22-00

From the Back of My Bible

Emolyn C. Lambert

BARBOUR
PUBLISHING, INC.
Uhrichsville, OH

ISBN 1-57748-164-X

All Scripture quotations are from the Authorized King James Version of the Bible.

Published by Barbour Publishing, Inc.
P.O. Box 719
Uhrichsville, Ohio 44683
http://www.barbourbooks.com

Member of the
Evangelical Christian
Publishers Association

Printed in the United States of America.

From the Back of My Bible

The Bible I carry was a gift from my mother in 1978. Over the years I have used the blank pages to jot down truths that have caught my attention and my soul. Those reminders are recorded here.

I take no credit for the contents. . .even the title is borrowed. Some are sermon notes, some are general comments, some are lyrics from songs. To those to whom I can give credit, I do. For those to whom I cannot, please forgive. Thanks to you all. Your words spoke to me.

I now hope God will use these words again to speak to your life.

Dedicated to my mom, Emolyn S. Crow,
the truest picture of Christ's love this side of glory.

*T*here is no *self-made* Christian.

We are the clay, and thou our potter;
and we all are the work of thy hand.
Isaiah 64:8

*Y*our life is the only Bible some will ever read.

Be thou an example of the believers,
in word, in conversation, in charity,
in spirit, in faith, in purity.
1 Timothy 4:12

"**K**now that I love you utterly."

Greater love hath no man than this,
that a man lay down his life for his friends.
John 15:13

When God seems far away—who moved?

Who shall separate us from the love of Christ?
Romans 8:35

We grow in grace but we don't grow in justification.
Our justification is settled.

By the righteousness of one the free gift
came upon all men unto justification of life.
Romans 5:18

There is no hope in this world apart from Him.

Which hope we have as an anchor of the soul,
both sure and stedfast.
Hebrews 6:19

*F*ive Results of Prayer:
Peace
Spiritual Growth
Walking in Fear of the Lord
We Will be Multiplied
Comfort and Encouragement by the Spirit

But let him ask in faith, nothing wavering.
James 1:6

My Goal:
To live every day as if Jesus died yesterday,
rose this morning,
and is coming again tomorrow.

Behold, I come quickly:
hold that fast which thou hast, that no man take thy crown.
Revelation 3:11

*H*e isn't Lord because we believe
or appointed Him so—
He *is* Lord.

And he hath. . .a name written,
KING OF KINGS, AND LORD OF LORDS.
Revelation 19:16

*N*o, Lord—a contradiction

Jesus saith. . .lovest thou me more than these?
He saith unto him, Yea, Lord.
John 21:15

*P*rayer acknowledges our dependence on God.

Yet the LORD will command his lovingkindness in the daytime,
and in the night his song shall be with me,
and my prayer unto the God of my life.
Psalm 42:8

$\mathcal{S}$AINT. . .someone the Light shines through

Let your light so shine before men,
that they may see your good works,
and glorify your Father which is in heaven.
Matthew 5:16

For what did you exchange your last 24 hours?

Wherefore do ye spend money for that which is not bread?
and your labour for that which satisfieth not?
Isaiah 55:2

The Bible tells us how to go to heaven and
how to be happy on the way!

Thou wilt show me the path of life:
in thy presence is fulness of joy.
Psalm 16:11

*G*od will *forgive* all sins—
He will not *excuse* any sin.

Saying, Blessed are they whose iniquities are forgiven,
and whose sins are covered.
Romans 4:7

*B*eautiful music
may be a miracle of the ear,
rather than of the voice.

Let me hear thy voice; for sweet is thy voice.
Song of Solomon 2:14

The love of God does not negate the wrath of God.

The great day of his wrath is come;
and who shall be able to stand?
Revelation 6:17

*H*e is too wise to make a mistake and
too loving to be unkind.

. . .that good, and acceptable, and perfect, will of God.
Romans 12:2

*R*ewards are judged by works.
Our destination is judged by faith.

There is therefore now no condemnation to them
which are in Christ Jesus,
who walk not after the flesh, but after the Spirit.
Romans 8:1

We are just one blink from eternity.

Whereas ye know not what shall be on the morrow.
For what is your life?
It is even a vapour, that appeareth for a little time,
and then vanisheth away.
James 4:14

We are as close to God as we choose to be. . .

Let us draw near with a true heart in full assurance of faith.
Hebrews 10:22

Who is motivated to serve God based on
seeing my obedience?

For your obedience is come abroad unto all men.
Romans 16:19

$\mathcal{W}$orry is a spasm of emotion. . . .

For God hath not given us the spirit of fear;
but of power, and of love, and of a sound mind.
2 Timothy 1:7

*G*od's acts reveal His person.

The heavens declare the glory of God;
and the firmament showeth his handiwork.
Psalm 19:1

We don't have to live in the power of sin,
but we will always live in its presence.

Let us lay aside every weight,
and the sin which doth so easily beset us.
Hebrews 12:1

*G*rieving the Holy Spirit—
thwarting His efforts in our lives and
not allowing Him full liberty

And grieve not the holy Spirit of God,
whereby ye are sealed unto the day of redemption.
Ephesians 4:30

*J*esus never measured a man by a moment;
we all have moments.
Jesus measures the make of the man.

—Dr. D. Bradley Price

Being justified by his grace . . .
Titus 3:7

What would happen if we all believed God?

. . . whosoever believeth in him should not perish,
but have everlasting life.
John 3:16

*S*atan can only divide;
only God unites.

Endeavoring to keep the unity of the Spirit in the bond of peace.
Ephesians 4:3

*D*eal with doubtful things by figuring out
what is right with them,
not by trying to figure out
exactly what is wrong!

If there be virtue, and if there be any praise,
think on these things.
Philippians 4:8

*S*in shows in:
time,
our body,
our character,
our conscience,
Day of Judgment

Awake to righteousness, and sin not.
1 Corinthians 15:34

*G*od is more interested in His glory
than in my circumstances.

Therefore glorify God in your body,
and in your spirit, which are God's.
1 Corinthians 6:20

What we *really* believe is reflected
in our personal conduct.

We should live soberly, righteously,
and godly, in this present world.
Titus 2:12

*I*nside the will of God there is no failure. . .
Outside the will of God there is no success.

He that doeth the will of God abideth for ever.
1 John 2:17

*A*ll trials and afflictions
have passed the judgment bar of God
before they are allowed to enter our lives.

The LORD gave, and the LORD hath taken away;
blessed be the name of the LORD.
Job 1:21

The deceitfulness of Satan links liberation to happiness.

Choosing rather to suffer affliction with the people of God,
than to enjoy the pleasures of sin for a season.
Hebrews 11:25

*D*oes God gain pleasure from what I am doing?

The Lord taketh pleasure in them that fear him,
in those that hope in his mercy.
Psalm 147:1

Salvation is free:
Lordship costs everything.

Whosoever he be of you that forsaketh not all that he hath,
he cannot be my disciple.
Luke 14:33

*J*esus did not die for everybody—
He died for each one of us.

While we were yet sinners, Christ died for us.
Romans 5:8

*P*eace is. . .
Understanding the oneness *of* God and
the oneness *with* God.

And the glory which thou gavest me I have given them;
that they may be one, even as we are one.
John 17:22

*P*eople don't go to heaven because of what they do—
it is because of *Whose* they are.

Ye are not your own.
1 Corinthians 6:19

*J*ust as the promised rains fell and
the earth split to gush forth water in Noah's Day,
so shall the eastern sky split to show the Son of Man in all
His glory in that final day. . .

—Dr. William Owens

And God shall wipe away all tears from their eyes;
and there shall be no more death, neither sorrow, nor crying,
neither shall there be any more pain.
Revelation 21:4

*O*bedience is the shortest road to blessing.

If they obey and serve him,
they shall spend their days in prosperity,
and their years in pleasures.
Job 36:11

*O*bedience to God begins in the heart.

Ye have purified your souls in obeying
the truth through the Spirit.
1 Peter 1:22

*F*aith is like a muscle. . .
The more exercise it gets,
The stronger it becomes.

. . . your faith is increased.
2 Corinthians 10:15

*T*rue joy comes from a heart of submissiveness.

Submit yourselves therefore to God.
James 4:7

*R*edeeming love has been my theme and shall be until I die.

I the LORD am thy Saviour and thy Redeemer.
Isaiah 60:16

Worship attributes worth to God.

O come, let us worship and bow down.
Psalm 95:6

The needs of life are truly a gift from Him.
They draw us away from self that
cannot meet the needs to Him
who meets all needs.
The abundant life is not needless.

But my God shall supply all your need
according to his riches in glory by Christ Jesus.
Philippians 4:19

*H*is grace does not on me depend—praise God!

God resisteth the proud, but giveth grace unto the humble.
James 4:6

We want God to grow us as tomatoes—
fast, pretty, but easily destroyed.
He wishes to grow us as oak trees—
slowly, patiently, sturdily, with long roots.

—Dr. William Owens

But grow in grace, and in the knowledge
of our Lord and Saviour Jesus Christ.
2 Peter 3:18

*J*esus Christ on Calvary was
the ultimate picture of non-retaliation.

But I say unto you, That ye resist not evil:
but whosoever shall smite thee on thy right cheek,
turn to him the other also.
Matthew 5:39

It is a mighty thing for a Christian to pray. . .
Not because we are mighty,
But because He is mighty.

Behold, God is. . .mighty in strength and wisdom.
Job 36:5

The gospel of Jesus Christ
is a trumpet in comparison
to the bugle gospel of the world—
theirs is a cheap imitation.

If any man preach any other gospel unto you
than that ye have received, let him be accursed.
Galatians 1:9

*J*esus Christ is able to change the human sequence
of events from life-death-judgment
to life-death-life.

For God sent not his Son into the world to condemn the world;
but that the world through him might be saved.
John 3:17

$\mathcal{S}$ubmission—
Yielding your will to someone else's
will so that God's will can be done.

Submitting yourselves one to another in the fear of God.
Ephesians 5:21

*A*ll that death can do to you is to bring you
into the immediate presence of the Savior.
Death, where is thy victory?

Jesus said unto him, Verily I say unto thee,
To day shalt thou be with me in paradise.
Luke 23:43

*H*e will never lead you where His
Grace will not sustain you.

My grace is sufficient for thee.
2 Corinthians 12:9

*S*ome folks' religion is more
"pomp and circumstance"
than "heart and soul."

Thou shalt love the Lord thy God with all thy heart,
and with all thy soul.
Matthew 22:37

If your cup is sweet, drink it with grace.
If your cup is bitter,
drink it in communion with Him.

—Oswald Chambers

In all their affliction he was afflicted.
Isaiah 63:9

*T*he gospel is like a lion—
you don't have to defend it. . .
just let it go.

Behold, the Lion of the tribe of Juda.
Revelation 5:5

We bless God when we return something
He has given to us—return it with your love.

Freely ye have received, freely give.
Matthew 10:8

*T*here is no shortage of Christians
with the will to go to heaven,

But there is a shortage
of those who will prepare.

Prepare to meet thy God.
Amos 4:12

*F*aith anticipates the fulfillment of God's promises.

Where is your faith?
. . .for he commandeth even the winds and water,
and they obey him.
Luke 8:25

*I*t is easy to give of your resources.
It is more difficult to give of yourself.

And though I bestow all my goods to feed the poor. . .
and have not charity, it profiteth me nothing.
1 Corinthians 13:3

*Y*ou either live in the presence
of faith or fear.

Yea, though I walk through the valley of the shadow of death,
I will fear no evil.
Psalm 23:4

M*iser* and *Miser*able
have the same root word!

Thou sayest, I am rich,
and increased with goods, and have need of nothing;
and knowest not that thou art wretched, and miserable.
Revelation 3:17

*C*hristians are not isolated
from the problems of the world,
but rather should be insulated
by the prayers of our church.

The effectual fervent prayer of a righteous man availeth much.
James 5:16

Would to God that I had never been born
than to lose one of these little ones. . .

James Dobson's grandmother's prayer about her own children.

It were better for him that a millstone were hanged about his neck,
and he cast into the sea,
than that he should offend one of these little ones.
Luke 17:2

$\mathcal{S}$in is agreeing with temptation.

God is faithful,
who will not suffer you to be tempted above that ye are able;
but will with the temptation also make a way to escape,
that ye may be able to bear it.
1 Corinthians 10:13

*H*is blood was used to forge the keys to heaven.

By his own blood he entered in once into the holy place,
having obtained eternal redemption for us.
Hebrews 9:12

Do I speak about Grace and practice Law?

Ye are not under the law, but under grace.
Romans 6:14

I am not all I ought to be,
But thank God I am not all I used to be.

. . . forgetting those things which are behind,
and reaching forth unto those things which are before.
Philippians 3:13

Fear is the evidence of my unbelief.

Perfect love casteth out fear.
1 John 4:18

I believe in the sun even when it is not shining,
I believe in love even when it is not felt,
I believe in God even when He is silent.

—Found on a cellar wall in Cologne, Germany after WWII

Now faith is the substance of things hoped for,
the evidence of things not seen.
Hebrews 11:1

*D*on't limit God by. . .
your muscles,
your pocketbook,
or your mind.

Great is the LORD, and greatly to be praised;
and his greatness is unsearchable.
Psalm 145:3

*P*rayer is fundamental,
not supplemental.

Pray without ceasing.
1 Thessalonians 5:17

*G*od's love prepares, not pampers.

We glory in tribulations also:
knowing that tribulation worketh patience.
Romans 5:3

Concurrence—God's almighty direction
and the casual power of my will.

Prepare ye the way of the Lord.
Mark 1:3

My goal will never exceed my conviction.

Let us run with patience the race that is set before us.
Hebrews 12:1

*O*nly one life twill soon be past.
Only what's done for Christ will last.

The fire shall try every man's work of what sort it is.
1 Corinthians 3:12

*T*urn your eyes upon Jesus.
Look full in His wonderful face.
And the things of earth will
grow strangely dim
in the light of His glory and grace.

Looking unto Jesus the author and finisher of our faith. . . .
Hebrews 12:2

Mercy is not receiving what is deserved.
Grace is receiving what is not deserved.

. . .The LORD God, merciful and gracious.
Exodus 34:6

My cross is where God's will and mine meet.

If any man will come after me, let him deny himself,
and take up his cross daily, and follow me.
Luke 9:23

*A*re we like Moses and in
our pseudo-devotion say:

Here am I, Lord.
Send Aaron.

I heard the voice of the Lord, saying, Whom shall I send,
and who will go for us? Then said I, Here am I; send me.
Isaiah 6:8

Not understanding the Trinity is akin to my not understanding living in a world with six dimensions.

His being is beyond the comfort of my mind's scope—
but if He were small enough for my mind,
He would not be large enough for my need.

Who is so great a God as our God?
Psalm 77:13

Pondering. . .Mary's ponderings were important
enough to be recorded in scripture.
We should ponder more.

And Mary said, My soul doth magnify the Lord,
And my spirit hath rejoiced in God my Saviour.
Luke 1:46–47

It will be worth it all when we see Jesus.
Life's trials will seem so small when we see Christ.

For now we see through a glass, darkly; but then face to face.
1 Corinthians 13:12

When temptation knocks at the door of your life,
let the Holy Spirit go to the door!

I also will keep thee from the hour of temptation.
Revelation 3:10

Everything in life is determined by
what we believe about God.

But as many as received him,
to them gave he power to become the sons of God,
even to them that believe on his name.
John 1:12

Without Christ, all is vanity.

I have seen all the works that are done under the sun;
and, behold, all is vanity and vexation of spirit.
Ecclesiastes 1:2

*I*f despair is the utter loss of hope,
then salvation is the utter joy of life.

The LORD is my strength and song,
and he is become my salvation.
Exodus 15:2

*S*ometimes God entrusts us with great sorrow. . . .

Surely he hath borne our griefs, and carried our sorrows.
Isaiah 53:4

*L*aw of Identical Harvest—
What we sow, we reap.

Whatsoever a man soweth, that shall he also reap.
Galatians 6:7

*A*nyone who doesn't believe in miracles
isn't a realist.

Then all the multitude kept silence,
. . .declaring what miracles and wonders God had wrought.
Acts 15:12

*O*ne day my faith will end in sight.

Now faith is the substance of things hoped for,
the evidence of things not seen.
Hebrews 11:1

The only values that merit your life's devotion
are those that death cannot change.

As for man, his days are as grass:
as a flower of the field, so he flourisheth.
. . .But the mercy of the LORD is from everlasting to everlasting.
Psalm 103:15, 17

*T*he greatest knowledge is to know the will of God.
The greatest endeavor is to do it.

He that doeth the will of God abideth for ever.
1 John 2:17

The world is the pattern of those without Christ.
He is our pattern.

So now also Christ shall be magnified in my body,
whether it be by life, or by death.
Philippians 1:20

My salvation is generated by the grace of God
and made secure by His faithfulness.

Great is thy faithfulness.
Lamentations 3:23

*I*f you find yourself going the wrong way,
remember that God allows U-turns.

The goodness of God leadeth thee to repentance.
Romans 2:4

$\mathcal{T}$he essence of sin is selfishness.

If we say that we have no sin, we deceive ourselves.
1 John 1:8

*G*od's anger is limited—
His love unbounded.

Many waters cannot quench love, neither can the floods drown it.
Song of Solomon 8:7

The high calling of Jesus Christ is not to be
compared with anything on this earth.

I press toward the mark for the prize
of the high calling of God in Christ Jesus.
Philippians 3:14

We will be enslaved one way or another.
The Bible presents a new master.

One is your Master, even Christ.
Matthew 23:10

The problem with unbelief is not familiarity,
but rather that we only half-hear the message.

He staggered not at the promise of God through unbelief.
Romans 4:20

There is one thing worse than waiting on God. . .
wishing you had.

For we through the Spirit wait. . .by faith.
Galatians 5:5

*J*eremiah's message from God:

I don't care how many times you have failed
and broken your vows—turn now
and I'll save and repair.

Turn, O backsliding children, saith the Lord;
for I am married unto you.
Jeremiah 3:14

We are to love others as we love ourselves:
unemotionally and spontaneously,
separate from sin and
unconditionally.

Charity never faileth.
1 Corinthians 13:8

The Lord never sent for a man who wasn't busy.

I heard the voice of the Lord, saying, Whom shall I send?
Isaiah 6:8

*J*esus Christ loves us—
not because of something in us,
but because of something in Him.

Herein is love, not that we loved God, but that he loved us.
1 John 4:10

*O*ur lifestyle is determined
by our level of commitment.

Know ye not that they which run in a race run all,
but one receiveth the prize? So run, that ye may obtain.
1 Corinthians 9:24

*T*here is peace in the middle
of my storm-tossed life.

For thou hast been a. . .refuge from the storm.
Isaiah 25:4

*A*ll I have seen teaches me to trust the Creator
for all I haven't seen.

Eye hath not seen, nor ear heard,
neither have entered into the heart of man,
the things which God hath prepared for them that love him.
1 Corinthians 2:9

*F*aith without works is dead.
Works without faith
are deceiving and hypocritical.

For as the body without the spirit is dead,
so faith without works is dead also.
James 2:26

*T*here is often a change of heart
between the time of surrender
and the time of service.

The children of Israel remembered not the LORD their God,
who had delivered them out of the hands
of all their enemies on every side.
Judges 8:34

To return evil for good is animal-like;
evil for evil is human-like;
good for evil is God-like.

But I say unto you, Love your enemies,
bless them that curse you, do good to them that hate you,
and pray for them which despitefully use you, and persecute you.
Matthew 5:44

*T*here are only a few inches
between a rut and an open grave.

But God will redeem my soul from the power of the grave.
Psalm 49:15

*D*eath is the way we get to heaven
before Jesus comes.

The righteous hath hope in his death.
Proverbs 14:32

We don't need to look at the world
and its situation to know He is coming.
He said He would and that's assurance.

I will come to you.
John 14:18

*Y*ou don't spell salvation D-O.
You spell it D-O-N-E.

He became the author of eternal salvation
unto all them that obey him.
Hebrews 5:9

There is no panic in heaven—just plans.

But the God of all grace,
who hath called us unto his eternal glory
by Christ Jesus. . .settle you.
1 Peter 5:10

*N*ever sacrifice the future
on the altar of the immediate.

But God said unto him, Thou fool,
this night thy soul shall be required of thee:
then whose shall those things be, which thou hast provided?
Luke 12:20

*J*esus Christ was never confused.

For God is not the author of confusion, but of peace.
1 Corinthians 14:33

*I*s it my *true* passion to honor Christ in all that I do?

Now unto the King eternal, immortal, invisible,
the only wise God, be honour and glory for ever and ever. Amen.
1 Timothy 1:17

The stone was not moved from the tomb
for Jesus to get out:
it was moved for us to see in.

And they found the stone rolled away from the sepulchre.
Luke 24:2

What kind of picture of my Lord
am I giving in my life?

The life which I now live in the flesh
I live by the faith of the Son of God,
who loved me, and gave himself for me.
Galatians 2:20

*P*rayerlessness is an indication of our self-sufficiency.

Praying always with all prayer and supplication in the Spirit.
Ephesians 6:18

*F*aith is that state of the soul
when the things of God
become glorious certainties.

If ye have faith as a grain of mustard seed,
ye shall say unto this mountain,
Remove hence to yonder place; and it shall remove;
and nothing shall be impossible unto you.
Matthew 17:20

*S*ometimes I'm up,
Sometimes I'm down,
But in my soul,
I'm heaven-bound.

In all these things we are more than conquerors
through him that loved us.
Romans 8:37

*D*id I do my best—
my *dead-level* best?

Jesus Christ could say so.

. . .Jesus Christ, and him crucified.
1 Corinthians 2:2

The colossal NO that men tried
to write across Jesus' life at Calvary,
on the third day at resurrection,
became an everlasting YES.

For if we have been planted together in the likeness of his death,
we shall be also in the likeness of his resurrection.
Romans 6:5

*I*f I can't unfold the petals of a rosebud
and make a flower,
what makes me think I can unfold the moments
of my life and make a flower?

Looking unto Jesus the author and finisher of our faith. . . .
Hebrews 12:2

A saint must have dogged determination
to be His disciple.

Let us run with patience the race that is set before us.
Hebrews 12:1

A man
or a woman
without Christ
is a hopeless equation.

I count all things but loss for the excellency
of the knowledge of Christ Jesus my Lord.
Philippians 3:8

roken hearts are sensitive to spiritual things.

He hath sent me to heal the brokenhearted.
Luke 4:18

*T*he question is not
"Who am I?"
but
"Whose am I?"

Because ye belong to Christ. . . he shall not lose his reward.
Mark 9:41

*P*atience. . .
Letting God be God.

. . .patience of hope in our Lord Jesus Christ.
1 Thessalonians 1:3

$\mathcal{S}$in is always present in the absence of faith.

Be not faithless, but believing.
John 20:27

We are to "come apart" on the Sabbath
so we don't come apart.

Hallow the sabbath day, to do no work therein.
Jeremiah 17:24

*Y*ou've got to feed the goodness in you
because the badness grows on its own.

But grow in grace,
and in the knowledge of our Lord and Saviour Jesus Christ.
2 Peter 3:18

*T*he sole pursuit of wealth and pleasure
is a goal unworthy of our calling.

For where your treasure is, there will your heart be also.
Luke 12:34

*T*oo often we sacrifice our joy for fun.

Jesus. . .who for the joy that was set before him endured the cross.
Hebrews 12:2

We are known by our deeds,
not by our creeds.

Study to show thyself approved unto God,
a workman that needeth not to be ashamed.
2 Timothy 2:15

*A*ll the hell we'll ever know is in this life.

And death and hell were cast into the lake of fire.
Revelation 20:14

When others see a shepherd boy,
God may see a king.

And the spirit of the Lord came upon David.
1 Samuel 16:13

*H*ave you ever needed Jesus Christ
and Him not show?

Lo, I am with you alway, even unto the end of the world.
Matthew 28:20

His salvation is sufficient for all,
but efficient only for those who believe.

Whosoever believeth in him should not perish,
but have everlasting life.
John 3:16

*Y*ou can't follow Christ at a distance.

My sheep hear my voice, and I know them, and they follow me.
John 10:27

ision comes from God and dawns on us.

For the vision is yet for an appointed time,
but at the end it shall speak, and not lie:
though it tarry, wait for it;
because it will surely come, it will not tarry.
Habbakuk 2:3

*Y*ou must understand Good Friday before
you can understand the open tomb
of Easter morning.

The Son of man must be delivered into the hands of sinful men,
and be crucified, and the third day rise again.
Luke 24:7

God has an amazing forgetfulness.

Blessed are they whose iniquities are forgiven,
and whose sins are covered.
Romans 4:7

*H*ow can I sin against His dying love for me?

O wretched man that I am!
who shall deliver me from the body of this death?
I thank God through Jesus Christ our Lord.
Romans 7:24-25

*M*ay there be nothing between my soul and the Savior.

Who shall separate us from the love of Christ?
Romans 8:35

We are to seek our joy in nothing but Christ.

Now the God of hope fill you with all joy and peace in believing.
Romans 15:13

*P*ain serves to make us homesick for heaven.

And God shall wipe away all tears from their eyes,
. . . neither shall there be any more pain.
Revelation 21:4

*A*ll things work together for good. . .
Just as an oak tree got strong by weathering
heat, cold, storm, rain, and hail,
the Christian becomes strong with
sorrow, joy, success, and failure.

And we know that all things work together
for good to them that love God,
to them who are the called according to his purpose.
Romans 8:28

The wilderness doesn't mean
we're out of God's will,
just detoured.

For in the wilderness shall waters break out,
and streams in the desert.
Isaiah 35:6

When the Holy Spirit speaks,
He does not mumble.

The Spirit itself maketh intercession for us.
Romans 8:26

I don't need to understand,
I just need to hold His hand.

If I take the wings of the morning,
and dwell in the uttermost parts of the sea;
Even there shall thy hand lead me,
and thy right hand shall hold me.
Psalm 139:9-10

There are only three kinds of people:
righteous,
unrighteous,
and
self-righteous.

The hope of the righteous shall be gladness.
Proverbs 10:28

*G*od's wrath is always designed to remove those things that blind us to His grace.

God resisteth the proud, and giveth grace to the humble.
1 Peter 5:5

We can either see the problem or see God.
Soldiers said Goliath was too big to hit.
David said he was too big to miss.

Great is the LORD.
Psalm 48:1

*T*he worst thing God could do
would be to leave us alone.

He hath said, I will never leave thee, nor forsake thee.
Hebrews 13:5

When I die, for all practical purposes,
Jesus will have returned.

Behold, I come quickly.
Revelation 22:7

When man continues to flaunt
his arrogance in God's face,
He either sends judgment
or revival.

Wilt thou not revive us again:
that thy people may rejoice in thee?
Psalm 85:6

There are no shortcuts to spiritual maturity.

Grow up into him in all things.
Ephesians 4:15

The greatest temptation in the wilderness
is the temptation to lower our standards.

And he was there in the wilderness forty days, tempted of Satan.
Mark 1:13

*J*esus Christ is the phenomenal change agent.
Nothing was the same when He left.

Behold, I make all things new.
Revelation 21:5

Cling to this world lightly.

Love not the world, neither the things that are in the world.
1 John 2:15

*F*aith produces miracles;
miracles don't produce faith.

Ye seek me, not because ye saw the miracles,
but because ye did eat of the loaves, and were filled.
John 6:26

*L*ove that goes up is worship,
love that goes out is affection,
love that stoops down is grace.

Keep yourselves in the love of God.
Jude 21

$\mathcal{L}$et's not be guilty of practicing
loveless truth and truthless love.

. . . speaking the truth in love.
Ephesians 4:15

I am determined before God
to be a Godly wife and mother.

That they may teach the young women to be sober,
to love their husbands, to love their children.
Titus 2:4

The world pities;
God has compassion.

His compassions fail not.
Lamentations 3:22

*E*ternity—
The harvest of our life.

God hath given to us eternal life, and this life is in his Son.
1 John 5:11

*T*he secret of life is not faith,
but His faithfulness.

Great is thy faithfulness.
Lamentations 3:23

*K*nee-ology is of more use than theology.

The effectual fervent prayer of a righteous man availeth much.
James 5:16

Why God wants our heart:
cleansing,
occupancy,
love's sake.

For God so loved the world. . .
John 3:16

The Lord wants our precious time,
not our spare time.

My times are in thy hand.
Psalm 31:15

*G*od's glory is rich and full;
man's glory is empty and vain.

Alleluia; Salvation, and glory, and honour,
and power, unto the Lord our God.
Revelation 19:1

*O*ur testament of the Christ
is evidence of our depravity.

But put ye on the Lord Jesus Christ,
and make not provision for the flesh,
to fulfil the lusts thereof.
Romans 13:14

Can you be truly grateful?

I will praise the name of God with a song,
and will magnify him with thanksgiving.
Psalm 69:30

*W*e are blood-bought children of the Father.

We are the children of God:
And if children, then heirs;
heirs of God, and joint-heirs with Christ.
Romans 8:16-17

*T*rouble tends to turn our attention towards trouble.
It should turn our attention towards
Jesus Christ.

Looking unto Jesus. . .
Hebrews 12:2

$\mathcal{S}$aint—

one whose sins have been covered
by the blood of Jesus Christ
and who strives daily
to do the will of his Father.

The blood of Jesus Christ his Son
cleanseth us from all sin.
1 John 1:7

*T*ithes and offerings are not financial transactions.
They are cheerful obedience
from a grateful heart.

Let him give; not grudgingly, or of necessity:
for God loveth a cheerful giver.
2 Corinthians 9:7

*G*od's wrath has fallen and burned at Calvary
and for those who kneel there,
there is no fear of the fire burning again.

There is therefore now no condemnation to
them which are in Christ Jesus.
Romans 8:1

$\mathcal{S}$ome folks react to life—saints respond.

We are more than conquerors through him that loved us.
Romans 8:37

*T*his life is a preface,
a boot camp for eternity.

He that hateth his life in this world
shall keep it unto life eternal.
John 12:25

*F*lattery elevates man.
The truth elevates God.

With flattering lips and with a double heart do they speak.
The LORD shall cut off all flattering lips.
Psalm 12:2-3

Christianity is not a religion,
It is a relationship.

We are to show the world it works.

I have called you friends.
John 15:15

The Holy Spirit never comes to us with the
indictment of sin without confronting
us also with the Savior.

Come, and let us return unto the Lord:
for he hath torn, and he will heal us;
he hath smitten, and he will bind us up.
Hosea 6:1

There will be no jealousy in heaven
because only One is worthy.

Thou art worthy, O Lord,
to receive glory and honour and power:
for thou hast created all things,
and for thy pleasure they are and were created.
Revelation 4:11

*G*od parted the Red Sea.
He just let Moses hold the stick.
What miracle am I watching happen before me
that God is allowing me to enjoy
while holding the stick?

And the Lord said unto Moses,
Stretch out thine hand over the sea.
Exodus 14:26

*G*od's spirit does not lead contrary
to His Word and does not
depend on my feelings.

Walk in the Spirit.
Galatians 5:16

*N*ever be confused.
Satan is the enemy.

Thou hast been. . .a strong tower from the enemy.
Psalm 61:3